IN BOOKS

Does W Trouble You?

Gerard Benson lives in Yorkshire with his wife, Cathy, and their cat, Chivers. He is a poet, story-teller, singer and performer, whose travels have taken him not only all over Great Britain, but to Africa, Europe, the USA and Canada. He has told stories to children in an African garden, a Channel Islands' zoo and a Thames cruiser, as well as schools, concert halls and theatres.

Gerard has had many jobs, amongst them sailor, actor, waiter, teacher, factory hand, washer-upper and university lecturer. He now writes, and gives readings and writing workshops to children and adults. In 1994 he was appointed poet-in-residence at Wordsworth's home, Dove Cottage. His *This Poem Doesn't Rhyme* won the 1991 Signal Poetry Award.

With two friends, Gerard started, and still runs, the Poems on the Underground scheme, placing poems on London tube trains. His children are now grown up and he has three grandchildren. He likes chess, reading, walking and music. He looks after a garden (sometimes), and he tries to write something every day.

D1146446

Other books by Gerard Benson

THE MAGNIFICENT CALLISTO
THIS POEM DOESN'T RHYME

Does W Trouble You?

Edited by Gerard Benson

Illustrated by Alison Forsythe

PUFFIN BOOKS

This book is dedicated to Oliver and Lucy,
rather late in life, but with much love

PUFFIN BOOKS

Published by the Penguin Group
Penguin Books Ltd, 27 Wrights Lane, London W8 5TZ, England
Penguin Books USA Inc., 375 Hudson Street, New York, New York 10014, USA
Penguin Books Australia Ltd, Ringwood, Victoria, Australia
Penguin Books Canada Ltd, 10 Alcorn Avenue, Toronto, Ontario, Canada M4V 3B2
Penguin Books (NZ) Ltd, 182–190 Wairau Road, Auckland 10, New Zealand

Penguin Books Ltd, Registered Offices: Harmondsworth, Middlesex, England

This collection first published by Viking 1994
Published in Puffin Books 1995
5 7 9 10 8 6

Text collection copyright © Gerard Benson, 1994
Illustrations copyright © Alison Forsythe, 1994
All rights reserved

The moral right of the author has been asserted

Printed in England by Clays Ltd, St Ives plc

CONTENTS

LETTERS PAGES

Dear Gerard

I am writing to inquire what you are choosing to put in your book of rhymed poetry. Will you be giving examples of all the different ways poems can rhyme? If so, it will be a very long book. Are there going to be any funny rhymes, like 'got 'em' and 'bottom'? If so, we will have to talk about it.

Yours sincerely

A. Puffin

Dear A. Puffin

Thanks for your letter. The book is ready now. Have a look at it yourself. I have included many kinds of rhyme, such as one-syllable rhymes, two-syllable rhymes and even three-syllable rhymes (which often sound funny). But there is nuffin, A. Puffin, quite like the rhyme you suggest.

Yours rhymingly

Gerard

Dear Gerard Benson

When I can't sleep, I think of rhymes in my head. Last night I thought of words that rhyme with 'right': light, bright, fright, fight, delight, sprite, bite, height. But I got all confused . . . and when I fell asleep I dreamt I was on a flight in a light kite shaped like an ammonite!

Yours sincerely

A. Girl

Dear A. Girl

All kites are light. They have to be. I think of rhymes in bed

10

too. *Last night was a failure: I couldn't think of a rhyme for dahlia.*

Yours

Gerard

Dear Gerard

You should have dreamt you were in Australia.

Yours

A. Girl

Dear Mr Benson

Why do people like rhyme?

Yours inquiringly

(Dr) Brian Speshu-List

Dear Doctor

Look at these pairs of words: tablet/sick; haddock/plate; heaven/wing. Now look at these: pill/ill; fish/dish; sky/fly. Doesn't something seem to happen when the words rhyme? Don't they seem to be pulled together and made to speak to each other?

Rhyme, when well done, works like a kind of magic, enriching the meanings of the words. But it must be used with skill and imagination. It isn't just a question of 'any old word that rhymes'.

Yours sincerely

Gerard Benson

Dear Mr Benson

There are one or two poems in your book that don't rhyme at all. I want my money back.

Yours demandingly

A. Cross-Reader

11

Dear Mr or Ms Cross-Reader

Oh yes they do. Look more carefully. The rhymes may be further apart than you think — or hidden inside the lines. Or the poet might be using half-rhymes, like 'rhyme/line/unseen' or 'caught/foot/rude'. Some poets prefer this to the 'noisy clang' of rhyme. But all the poems rhyme, though it's not always easy to see (and hear) how.

Yours

Gerard Benson

Dear Gerard Benson

I like words that rhyme with themselves, like picnic and Zulu and ragbag and tingling.

Yours

Roy Boy

Dear Roy

So do I. Have a look at Cicely Herbert's poem. It's full of words like that, and they all begin with H!

Yours

GeeBee

Dear Gerard

Who is this Aunt Effie? I know you have no aunt with that name.

Your indignant cousin

Vincent

Dear Vincent

Aunt Effie is not just my aunt. She's everybody's aunt. It is

the name that was used by a popular Victorian children's
writer, Jane Euphemia Browne.

Your know-all cousin

Gerard

Dear Mr Benson

The spelling in Marjory Fleming's sonnet is a disgrace.

Yours sincerley

Mr Spellrite

Dear Mr Spellrite

Little Marjory Fleming was eight years old when she died in
1811. Although I have corrected the spelling of adult poets
where necessary, I've left Marjory's as she wrote it because I
think children will like to see exactly how a little girl wrote a
poem all those years ago. As it happens, it isn't really a
sonnet either.

Yours sincerely

Gerard Benson

Dear Editor

I am an artist and mathematician. I have noticed that many
poems have quite beautiful and complicated *patterns* of
rhyme.

Yours

(Ms) Algebra Paintbrush

Dear Ms Paintbrush (or may I call you Algebra?)

I'm glad you noticed that. Some rhyme patterns, such as
couplets, are very simple. (You, as a mathematician, will
understand why we call these rhymes AABBCC, etc.) Some
are a little more complex, like ABAB, ABCB, or ABBA. And

13

some are very intricate indeed. Some poems have no set rhyme pattern (take a look at 'Somewhere in the Sky').

Yours

Gerard Benson

Dear Mr Benson

Poems are meant to be read, enjoyed and understood for what they are. Who cares how they are made?

Yours ferociously

A. Poetry-Lover

Dear A. Poetry-Lover

The poets care how poems are made. What the poem is saying is, of course, important. But with poetry the sound it makes can be just as important. Rhythm is even more telling than rhyme. Many readers read with their ears as well as their eyes. In fact, it's a good idea to read poetry aloud, whenever possible.

Yours sincerely

Gerard Benson

Dear Gerard

Your tea's ready.

Yours lovingly

Mrs C. Benson

Dear Mrs Benson

Good. I'd just finished this introduction, anyway. I just hope the readers get as much pleasure from reading these wonderful poems as I did in choosing them.

Yours thirstily

G.

Various ways to rhyme

The King sent for his wise men all
  To find a rhyme for W.
When they had thought a good long time
But could not think of a single rhyme,
'I'm sorry,' said he, 'to trouble you.'

                              James Reeves

The Diners in the Kitchen

Our dog Fred
Et the bread.

Our dog Dash
Et the hash.

Our dog Pete
Et the meat.

Our dog Davy
Et the gravy.

Our dog Toffy
Et the coffee.

Our dog Jake
Et the cake.

Our dog Trip
Et the dip.

And – the worst,
From the first –

Our dog *Fido*
Et the pie-dough.

James Whitcomb Riley

Sheridan's Calendar

January snowy,
February flowy,
March blowy,

April showery,
May flowery,
June bowery,

July moppy,
August croppy,
September poppy,

October breezy,
November wheezy,
December freezy.

Anon.

Interlaced rhyme: ABAB

Tewkesbury Road

It is good to be out on the road, and going one
    knows not where,
  Going through meadow and village, one knows
    not whither nor why;
Through the grey light drift of the dust, in the keen
    cool rush of the air,
  Under the flying white clouds, and the broad blue
    lift of the sky;

And to halt at the chattering brook, in the tall green
    fern at the brink
  Where the harebell grows, and the gorse, and the
    fox-gloves purple and white;
Where the shy-eyed delicate deer troop down to the
    pools to drink,
  When the stars are mellow and large at the coming
    on of the night.

O! to feel the warmth of the rain, and the homely
    smell of the earth,
  Is a tune for the blood to jig to, a joy past power
    of words;
And the blessed green comely meadows seem all
    a-ripple with mirth
  At the lilt of the shifting feet, and the dear wild cry
    of the birds.

John Masefield

Frutta Di Mare

I am a sea shell flung
Up from the ancient sea;
Now I lie here, among
Roots of a tamarisk tree;
No one listens to me.

I sing to myself all day
In a husky voice, quite low,
Things the great fishes say
And you must need to know;
All night I sing just so.

But lift me from the ground,
And hearken at my rim;
Only your sorrow's sound
Amazed, perplexed and dim,
Comes coiling to the brim;

For what the wise whales ponder
Awaking out from sleep,
The key to all your wonder,
The answers of the deep,
These to myself I keep.

Geoffrey Scott

Racing the wind

eyes staring
nostrils flaring

feet dancing
legs prancing

manes flowing
tails blowing

hooves pacing
horses racing

Moira Andrew

How the Daughters Come Down at Dunoon

How do the daughters
Come down at Dunoon?
Daintily,
Tenderly,
Fairily,
Gingerly,
Glidingly,
Slidingly,
Slippingly,
Skippingly,
Trippingly,
Clippingly,
Bumpingly,
Thumpingly,
Stumpingly,
Clumpingly,
Starting and bolting,
And darting and jolting,
And tottering and staggering,
And lumbering and slithering,
And hurrying and scurrying,
And worrying and flurrying,
And rushing and leaping and crushing and creeping;
Feathers a-flying all – bonnets untying all –
Petticoats rapping and flapping and slapping all,
Crinolines flowing and blowing and showing all
Balmorals, dancing and glancing, entrancing all;
Feats of activity –
Nymphs on declivity –
Mothers in extacies –
Fathers in vextacies –

22

Lady-loves whisking and frisking and clinging on
True-lovers puffing and blowing and springing on,
Dashing and clashing and shying and flying on,
Blushing and flushing and wriggling and giggling on,
Teasing and pleasing and squeezing and wheezing on,
Everlastingly falling and bawling and sprawling on,
Tumbling and rumbling and grumbling and
                                  stumbling on,
          Any fine afternoon,
          About July or June –
          That's just how the Daughters
          Come down at Dunoon!

                              H. Cholmondeley Pennell

Conversation

'Ha! Taking a week off?'
'Heart aching; a wee cough.'

Gerard Benson

Monorhyme – only one rhyme sound

The Ruling Power

Gold! Gold! Gold! Gold!
Bright and yellow, hard and cold,
Molten, graven, hammered and rolled;
Heavy to get, and light to hold;
Hoarded, bartered, bought and sold,
Stolen, borrowed, squandered, doled;
Spurned by the young, but hugged by the old,
To the very verge of the churchyard mould;
Price of many a crime untold;
Gold! Gold! Gold! Gold!
Good or bad, a thousandfold!

Thomas Hood

The Wide-Eyed Stride Poem

Slide down a shining snake,
Hide in mighty trees,
Side with the Indians,
Stride across the seas.

Tried worms for breakfast,
Dyed bright blue;
Fried spider dumplings in
Dried banana stew.

Shied at the coconuts,
Eyed up the cost;
Sighed when I won a prize,
Cried when I lost.

Pried into secrets,
Lied about my age,
Tied up all my enemies,
Died in a cage.

Pride of very hungry lions,
Guide dogs for the blind,
Pied Piper of Hamelin and the
Bride of Frankenstein.

Wide beaches where the white
Tide-line gleams:
Ride a golden dragon and
Glide into your dreams.

Tony Charles

Internal Rhyme

Do you know, when you eat there are thirty-two feet
      of interior tubing to deal with it?
Allow this to grapple, let's say with an apple –
      it may or may not have the peel with it –
Just imagine the pippin beginning its trip in
      the throat, which adjoins the oesophagus
(It has quitted the mouth on its way to the south,
      like a corpse in a shifting sarcophagus);
And think what befalls as those rubbery walls
      embrace it and knead it between 'em;
What knowledge it learns as it slithers and turns
      and lands up in the dark duodenum –
A minimal hummock, it's been through the stomach –
      reduced, so I'm told, by the acid,
Which gives it a spray as it moves on its way,
      and renders it mushy and placid . . .

Well, you're getting the picture, but, risking the
                         stricture
      that stories once started should finish,
I propose to omit what is waiting for it
      as its size and its structure diminish.
If I pass unrecorded the subsequent sordid
      adventures that form the diurnal
Dispersion achieved, you should not feel aggrieved –
      I'm confined to the strictly internal.

Mary Holtby

Zoe's Ear-rings

She bought 'em in the autumn
After spotting 'em in Nottingham.
She took 'em home to Cookham
And she put 'em in a drawer

Till May came and the day came
When she wore 'em down to Shoreham,
But *nobody* was for 'em
So she wore 'em nevermore . . .

Till the wedding of her sister
To a mister out at Bicester,
Name of Jimmy, who said, '*Gimme*,'
So without 'em she went home,

But she nipped back down to nick 'em
For a knees-up in High Wycombe,
For an evening quite near Chevening
And a dawn at Kilmalcolm.

They were in 'er for a dinner
Which was excellent, in Pinner,
And another one, a cracker,
In Majacca – that's in Spain –

Then she popped 'em on in Haddenham
And didn't feel too bad in 'em:
She felt in 'em, in Cheltenham,
Just as right as rain.

They looked smart on in Dumbarton,
They looked wizard on the Lizard,
They looked corking down in Dorking
And incredible in Crewe.

When she wore 'em into Rugely
They impressed the people hugely,
While in Fordham folk adored 'em,
And they *loved* 'em in West Looe!

The citizens of Kettering
Had never seen a better ring,
In fact no better pair of 'em –
'Take care of 'em!' they cried.

Then she slithered into Lytham with 'em,
Shaking out a rhythm with 'em,
Wobb-er-ling and jogg-er-ling
Her head from side to side.

Folk in Preston thought the best 'un
Was the right 'un. In New Brighton
And in Sefton, though, the *left* 'un
Was the one they favoured more,

While in Greenham, when they'd seen 'em,
They said, 'How to choose between 'em?
What one praises in its brother,
In the *other* one is for!'

Then she tried 'em with new make-up
On a sponsored run round Bacup,
And at Norwich for a porridge-
Eating contest which she won,

But, spilling 'em in Gillingham,
Her lobes felt light in Willingham,
And nothing else is filling 'em,
So now

The poem's

Done!

Kit Wright

Frying Panic

Oh once when my dad tried frying, pan
ic! Mum threw a proper wobbly, curt
ains blazed. 'You're so flaming stupid, man
age food? You're a prat, Dad! See that skirt
ing board? It's as black as soot! A char
ming chump, that is all you are, a bum
bling bungler!' He always looks a star
tled stoat, and he gets these fits of mum
bles, when they are both in giant wig
gies. Dad went outside and kicked the doors
tep. Mum? In the smoke, we watched her jig
gle plates in a fury, throwing sauce
rs.

Bill Greenwell

Desperation sets in. The poet invents words to rhyme

Eletelephony

Once there was an elephant
Who tried to use the telephant —
No! no! I mean an elephone
Who tried to use the telephone —
(Dear me! I am not certain quite
That even now I've got it right.)

Howe'er it was, he got his trunk
Entangled in the telephunk;
The more he tried to get it free,
The louder buzzed the telephee —
(I fear I'd better drop this song
Of elephop and telephong!)

Laura Richards

More desperation. The poet alters the spelling

An old couple living in Gloucester

An old couple living in Gloucester
Had a beautiful girl but they loucester!
   She fell from a yacht
   And never the spacht
Could be found where the cold waves had toucester.

Anon.

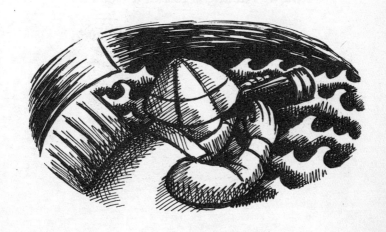

Utter desperation. The poet changes the facts to get her rhyme

Sonnet
(To Pug, a Pet Monkey)

O lovely O most charming pug
Thy gracefull air & heavenly mug
The beauties of his mind do shine
And every bit is shaped so fine
Your very tail is most devine
Your teeth is whiter then the snow
You are a great buck & a bow
Your eyes are of so fine a shape
More like a christains then an ape
His cheeks is like the roses blume
Your hair is like the ravens plume
His noses cast is of the roman
He is a very pretty weomen
I could not get a rhyme for roman
And was oblidged to call it weoman

Marjory Fleming

Portrait gallery

'Father and Mother and Me
Sister and Auntie say
All the people like us are We
And everyone else is They.'

Rudyard Kipling

Wha Me Mudder Do

Mek me tell you wha me mudder do
wha me mudder do
wha me mudder do

Me mudder pound plantain mek fufu
Me mudder catch crab mek calaloo stew

Mek me tell you wha me mudder do
wha me mudder do
wha me mudder do

Me mudder beat hammer
Me mudder turn screw
she paint chair red
then she paint it blue

Mek me tell you wha me mudder do
wha me mudder do
wha me mudder do

Me mudder chase bad-cow
with one 'Shoo'
she paddle down river
in she own canoe
Ain't have nothing
dat me mudder can't do
Ain't have nothing
dat me mudder can't do

Mek me tell you

Grace Nichols

37

Breakfast

My daddy reads at breakfast, He holds THE TIMES up high.
We sometimes hear a mutter, And sometimes catch a sigh.
We wonder what he's up to Behind that screen of print
It must be fascinating, but We've not the smallest hint.
If one of us should ask him, He says it's 'world affairs'
But Mummy says it's cricket, Or boring stocks and shares.
Then when he folds his paper And grabs his things to go.
His egg and toast are eaten, Quite how, we'll never know.
So, when I need permission For something I have planned.
I don't ask him at teatime – For then he'd understand –
I wait until it's breakfast, Then make my special plea.
And if he mumbles 'Mmmm', That's good enough for me!

Noel Petty

Tidying up

Put the shot putt
In the sports hut, and
Slam the sports hut door shut.
O K –
That's the shot putt
Put in the hut
Shut up safely for the night.
All right,
Stick the javelin in the equipment bin,
The vaulting pole in the hidey hole,
Slide the rackets in their packets,
Hide the cricket stumps and running pumps,
The shuttlecocks and smellysocks,
Take the shiny shorts across the courts
And put the vaulting vests inside their chests,
Then store the brightly bouncing batting balls
Inside the sports hall.
Er . . . That's all.

Simon Pitt

You will soon get warm as you run up and down

The teacher's in that cute
sporty bright pink tracksuit

and under it
you know she's got on
her thermal shorts
and Damart longjohns,
her thermal shirt
and thermal vest
like for an assault
on Everest.

Have you guessed?
Have you guessed?

Well, this'll help you crack it:
she's putting on her sheepskin jacket,

her hands are mittens
round a mug of tea
and she stamps her feet
continually

while the boys and girls
run out for sports
in thin white shirts
and thin white shorts

their thin white arms
and thin white legs
like bits of string
with knots in
shivering
and as they do

turning blue.

Peter Sansom

from **The Poet and the Fly**

Old Man's Song

    Catch 'em alive! Gentlemen, I've
Here such a dose as no fly can survive.
    House-fly, bluebottle,
    Garden-fly – what'll
Save him when once he's got this in his throttle?
Let e'en a wasp dip his nose in the mixture,
Spread on a plate, and that wasp is a fixture.
    Buy, buy; give it a try;
Don't be put down by a poor little fly.
    Who'll purchase any? Only a penny
Kills you them all, if it's ever so many.

C.S. Calverley

The Sniffle

In spite of her sniffle,
Isabel's chiffle.
Some girls with a sniffle
Would be weepy and tiffle;
They would look awful
Like a rained-on waffle,
But Isabel's chiffle
In spite of her sniffle.
Her nose is more red
With a cold in her head,
But then, to be sure,
Her eyes are bluer.
Some girls with a snuffle
Their tempers are uffle,
But when Isabel's snivelly
She's snivelly civilly,
And when she is snuffly
She's perfectly luffly.

Ogden Nash

Full Moon

She was wearing the coral taffeta trousers
Someone had brought her from Isfahan,
And the little gold coat with pomegranate blossoms,
And the coral-hafted feather fan;
But she ran down a Kentish lane in the moonlight,
And skipped in the pool of the moon as she ran.

She cared not a rap for all the big planets,
For Betelgeuse or Aldebaran,
And all the big planets cared nothing for her,
That small impertinent charlatan,
But she climbed on a Kentish stile in the moonlight,
And laughed at the sky through the sticks of her fan.

Victoria Sackville-West

Who?

Who dresses in rags, though could be rich;
And may sleep sometimes in a ditch?
Whose hands and face are grained with pitch,
And has a hooked and running snitch,
And very often seems to itch?
Who owns a black-coated, red-eyed bitch,
And yet from hag to cat may switch?
Who makes your hair rise up and twitch,
Standing unmoving in a niche?
Who dances round without a stitch?
Whose grandad cured the Czarevitch?
– Madam Malibran, the witch.

Roy Fuller

simple tings

(For Miss Adlyn and Aunt Vida)

de simple tings of life, mi dear
de simple tings of life

she rocked the rhythms in her chair
brushed a hand across her hair
miles of travel in her stare

de simple tings of life

ah hoe mi corn
an de backache gone
plant mi peas
arthritis ease

de simple tings of life

leaning back
she wiped an eye
read the rain signs
in the sky
evening's ashes
in a fireside

de simple tings of life.

Jean 'Binta' Breeze

Granny Granny Please Comb my Hair

Granny Granny please comb
my hair
you always take your time
you always take such care

You put me on a cushion
between your knees
you rub a little coconut oil
parting gentle as a breeze

Mummy Mummy
she's always in a hurry-hurry
rush
she pulls my hair
sometimes she tugs

But Granny
you have all the time
in the world
and when you're finished
you always turn my head and say
'Now who's a nice girl'

Grace Nichols

from Tommy Big-Eyes

'And Tommy had a fiddle too,
And I don't know what there was he couldn't do
With yonder fiddle, the way it'd mock
Everything – it'd crow like a cock,
It'd hoot like a donkey, it'd moo like a cow;
It'd cry like a baby, it'd grunt like a sow,
Or a thrush, or a pigeon, or a lark, or a linnet –
You'd really thought they were livin' in it.
But the tunes he was playin' – that was the thing –
Like squeezin' honey from the string:
Like milking a fiddle – no jerks, no squeaks –
And the tears upon the mistress' cheeks.
And sometimes he'd play a dance – and what harm!
But she wouldn't have it upon the farm,
The mistress wouldn't – dancing I mean –
It didn't matter so much for the playing:
But she'd often stop him, and ask would he change
To a nice slow tune, and Tommy would range
Up and down the strings, and slither
Into the key; and then he'd feather
The bow very fine, and a sort of a hum,
Like a bee round a flower, and out it'd come –
"Old Robin Gray" or "The Lover's Ghost" –
That's the two she liked most.'

T.E. Brown

Pembroke

There once was a poet of Damn!

There once was a poet of Pembroke
Who said 'Damn' whenever his Damn!!

There once was a poet of Pembroke
Who said 'Damn' whenever his pen broke,
   So he'd get a new pen
   Start all over a-Damn!!!

There once was a poet of Pembroke
Who said 'Damn' whenever his pen broke,
   So he'd get a new pen,
   Start all over again,
That Determined young poet of . . .

                        Oh DAMN!!!!

                  William Bealby-Wright

The Gymnast

Willie was proud of his handstand.
He did it on the local grandstand,
He did it on the bandstand
And he did it on the sands and
He did it so much in the sun
That his feet got overdone
But he never got his hands tanned.

                Alistair Samson

Places and their people

By clinging to the chimbley,
You could see across to Wembley
  If it wasn't for the 'ouses in between.

                    Edgar Bateman

Banana and Mackerel

O look ow markit full –
ow markit of London pull
field crop them come a-follah we
across Caribbean sea.

Look pon white and yellow yam,
pon ripe plantain and green Lacatan.
Look pon big, deep-flesh avocados,
ackee and red sweet potatoes.

Lord, people-food come a Englan
and stop Westindian food ration.
Back-home flavours deh yah
like all fish, fowl and fruit colour.

Yu can get yu spices and sorrel,
can av bwoil banana and mackerel.
O fishin and cuttin and pickin follah we
across Caribbean sea.

James Berry

Composed upon Westminster Bridge
3 September 1802

Earth has not anything to show more fair:
Dull would he be of soul who could pass by
A sight so touching in its majesty:
This City now doth like a garment wear
The beauty of the morning; silent, bare,
Ships, towers, domes, theatres, and temples lie
Open unto the fields, and to the sky;
All bright and glittering in the smokeless air.
Never did sun more beautifully steep
In his first splendour, valley, rock or hill;
Ne'er saw I, never felt, a calm so deep!
The river glideth at his own sweet will:
Dear God! the very houses seem asleep;
And all that mighty heart is lying still!

William Wordsworth

On the Footpath at Old Leigh

Spring morning, misty dawning,
Sunshine forming, day warming.
Seagulls gliding, walkers striding,
Sea slip-slapping, riggings tapping.
Boatmen spraying, children playing,
Paintpots spilling, buckets filling,
Varnish dripping, castles tipping,
Mugs of tea, shouts of glee,
Zip and zest, peace and rest,
Stand and stare, lose your care
And strain . . .

Distant drumming, wires start humming,
Rails singing, fence swinging,
Seagulls fleeing danger seeing,
Air thundering, children wondering,
Houses shaking, footpath quaking,
Pistons snoring, motor roaring,
Wheels gyrating and rotating,
Clitter clatter, eardrums shatter,
Wits scaring, eyes staring,
Horn blaring, sense tearing –
TRAIN!

Katie Mallett

Souvenir from Weston-Super-Mare

Moving in a bunch like creeping hands
    the donkeys, prised from their hay,
cross the day's backdrop again: cloud, tide, mud
    cement the scene grey.

I scoop away. I build. I mould – the oil's
    good for adhesion. There, that
can do for the necessary moat,
    and look! A *sand-cat*!

Ears, nose, paws straight from Egypt. And still
    ten minutes before the bus.
We look back from the top of the wall.
    Long drawn out after us

a family comes breasting the wind.
    It'll be right in their track.
The boy spots it first, running ahead.
    He goes running back

to fetch the others. They cluster and point,
    looking up and down the strand
before the wind detaches them again.
    He waits. Their backs turned,

he drops to his knees, he strokes the sand fur.
    Come on – five past the bus leaves!
Dodging the weaving cars we race the station
    clock's hands light as thieves.

Libby Houston

from A Nocturnal Sketch

Even is come; and from the dark Park, hark,
The signal of the setting sun – one gun!
And six is sounding from the chime, prime time
To go and see the Drury Lane Dane slain.

Now thieves to enter for your cash, smash, crash,
Past drowsy Charley, in a deep sleep, creep,
But frightened by Policeman B3, flee,
And while they're going, whisper low, 'No go!'

Now puss, while folks are in their beds, treads leads
And sleepers waking, grumble – 'Drat that cat!'
Who in the gutter caterwauls, squalls, mauls
Some feline foe, and screams in shrill ill-will.

Thomas Hood

Uphill . . .

The endless hill appears to grow
Steeper yet, and so I go
Slower still, at last so slow
I seem to move through drifts of snow,
Or through a sludge of baker's dough,
And yet the pedals still go round.
I stay upright, although the ground
Doesn't make the slightest sound
Against the tyres' laborious touch.
I doubt if I can pedal much
Longer now. I heave and press
And grunt and groan in my distress,
And yet the pedals still revolve,
And somehow strengthen my resolve
To reach the summit of the hill,
Achieved at last through strength of will
Rather than through power or skill.
Once there I flop upon the earth
And take deep breaths for all I'm worth,
Till energy returns once more;
And then I rise, and see before

My feet the countryside unfold,
Fields of green and fields of gold,
Dark stains of shadows, cast by trees
So small you could with perfect ease
Pluck them as you would pick flowers.
I could stay gazing here for hours
But soon, alas, I have to go.
Of one thing I am certain though,
And this is what it is: I know
That all the effort, sweat and pain
Were not endured by me in vain:
The pleasure that this view provides
Is worth a dozen painful rides.

Vernon Scannell

The Morris Dancers

Hey! who comes here all-along,
With bagpiping and drumming?
'Tis the Morris dance a-coming.
Come, come, ladies, come ladies out;
O! come, come quickly,
And see how trim they dance, how trim and trickly.

Hey! there again, there again; hey ho there again,
Hey! there again, how the bells they shake it,
Now for our town once, and take it.
Soft awhile, not so fast; they melt them:
What ho Piper! Piper be hanged awhile:
Knave, seest not the dancers how they swelt them?
Out there awhile you come: I say you are too far in;
There, give the hobby horse more room to play in.

Thomas Morley

The Dancer

The tall dancer dances
With slowly-taken breath:
In his feet music,
And on his face death.

His face is a mask,
It is so still and white:
His withered eyes shut,
Unmindful of light.

The old fiddler fiddles
The Merry 'Silver Tip'
With softly-beating foot
And laughing eye and lip.

And round the dark walls
The people sit and stand,
Praising the art
Of the dancer of the land.

But he dances there
As if his kin were dead:
Clay in his thoughts,
And lightning in his tread.

Joseph Campbell

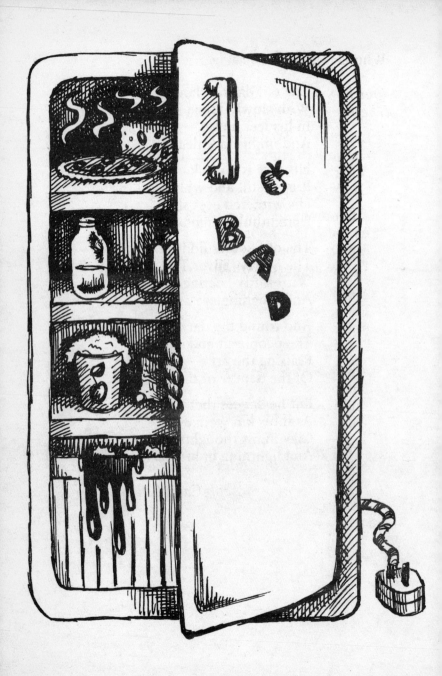

Who Unplugged the Fridge?

Quick! Somebody call the Germ Exterminator.
There are nasty things lurking in our refrigerator.

Like a yellow milk bottle
Half full of stinking gunge
And the chisel-breaking remnants
Of a dried-up lemon sponge.

A lump of pink blancmange
As tough as a boot heel.
A pizza that is hard enough
To use as a pram wheel.

A melon that has shrivelled
To the size of a pea.
And a cheese whose 'sell-by date'
Is ancient history.

A bag of liquid lettuce
That moves when you poke it.
And furry-topped yoghurt
That purrs when you stroke it.

Quick! Somebody call the Germ Exterminator.
There are nasty things lurking in our refrigerator.

John Coldwell

Wet Playtime

hungry chatter
friendly chatter
pitter patter
what's the matter?
tattered textbooks
skim like skates
bad boys batter
last week's mates
watch the rain
just drench the playground
blowing paper
round and round
here inside
the jigsaws clatter
eat those crisps
they'll make you fatter
drop your juice
and dodge the splatter
teacher's coming
quick let's scatter
pitter patter
nitter natter
friendly chatter
what's the matter?

Dave Ward

The Proper Way to Leave a Room

The Proper Way to Leave a Room
Is not to Plunge it into Gloom;
Just Make a Joke before you Go
And then Escape before They Know.

Gelett Burgess

Cross-Patch

Cross-patch
Draw the latch,
Sit by the fire and spin;
Take a cup
And drink it up,
Then call your neighbours in.

Anon.

Food for thought

He thought he saw a Rattlesnake
  That questioned him in Greek,
He looked again and saw it was
  The Middle of Next Week.

Lewis Carroll

Fish Pie with Orchestra

You can scrabble with a scallop
      or a lobster,
you can tussle with a mussel
      or a crab;
you can whet your appetite
      with whelks or winkles,
or dangle from the pier
      for plaice or dab.

You can hear the noisy
      oyster-catcher fishing,
the ringing of the curlew's
      long 'coo-lee';
the tapping of the turnstone
      seeking supper,
the whispered song sung by
      the rolling sea.

Judith Nicholls

Calendar Poem

Januar:	By this fire I warm my hands.
Februar:	And with my spade I delve my lands.
Marche:	Here I set my things to spring,
Aprile:	And here I hear the fowls sing.
Maii:	I am as light as bird on bough.
Junii:	And I weed my corn well enough.
Julii:	With my scythe my meadow I mow.
Auguste:	And here I shear my corn full low.
September:	With my flail I earn my bread,
October:	And here I sow my wheat so red.
November:	At Martinsmas I kill my swine.
December:	And at Christmas I drink red wine.

Anon. (Medieval)

Ozymandias

I met a traveller from an antique land
Who said: Two vast and trunkless legs of stone
Stand in the desert . . . Near them, on the sand,
Half sunk, a shattered visage lies, whose frown,
And wrinkled lip, and sneer of cold command,
Tell that its sculptor well those passions read
Which yet survive, stamped on these lifeless things,
The hand that mocked them and the heart that fed;
And on the pedestal these words appear:
'My name is OZYMANDIAS, king of kings;
Look on my works, ye Mighty, and despair!'
Nothing beside remains. Round the decay
Of that colossal wreck, boundless and bare
The lone and level sands stretch far away.

Percy Bysshe Shelley

from **To James Smith**

Just now I've taen the fit o' rhyme,
My barmie noddle's working prime,
My fancie yerkit up sublime
            Wi' hasty summon;
Hae ye a leisure-moment's time
            To hear what's comin?

Some rhyme a neebor's name to lash;
Some rhyme (vain thought!) for needfu' cash;
Some rhyme to court the country clash,
            An' raise a din;
For me, an aim I never fash;
            I rhyme for fun.

The star that rules my luckless lot,
Has fated me the russet coat,
An' damn'd my fortune to the groat;
            But, in requit,
Has blest me with a random shot
            O' country wit.

Robert Burns

Healthfood Soup

Take a robin's leg
(Mind, the drumstick merely);
    Put it in a tub
Filled with water nearly;
    Set it out of doors,
In a place that's shady;
    Let it stand a week
(Three days if for a lady);
    Drop a spoonful of it
In a five-pail kettle,
    Which may be made of tin
Or any baser metal;
    Fill the kettle up,
Set it on a boiling,
    Strain the liquor well,
To prevent its oiling;
    One atom add of salt,
For the thickening one rice kernel,
    And use to light the fire
The Homœopathic Journal.
    Let the liquor boil
Half an hour, no longer
    (If 'tis for a man
Of course you'll make it stronger).
    Should you now desire
That the soup be flavoury,
    Stir it once around
With a stalk of savory.

When the broth is made,
Nothing can excel it:
    Then three times a day
Let the patient *smell* it.
    If he chance to die,
Say 'twas Nature did it:
    If he chance to live,
Give the soup the credit.

Anon.

Herb the Superb's Hound the Sound Poem

Hells bells! What a hubbub
Hotchpotch, hubble bubble!
Here we go, hugger mugger
Hurtle down the helter skelter.

    Hairy canary
    (much too scary)

Habdabs and heeby jeebies
Hanky panky! Hoity toity
Hoi polloi, hurly burly
Honky tonk, hurdy gurdy

    Hi 'n' dri
    (wish I could fly)

Hustle 'n' bustle, hurry 'n' scurry
Hither 'n' thither, hickory dickory
Hocus pocus, hippety hoppety
Harum scarum, higgledy piggledy

    Huff 'n' puff
    (that's enuff)

Cicely Herbert

Sausage and Mash

If there's a dish
For which I wish
More frequent than the rest,
If there's a food
On which I brood
When starving or depressed,
If there's a thing that life can give
Which makes it worth our while to live,
If there's an end
On which I'd spend
My last remaining cash,
It's sausage, friend,
It's sausage, friend,
It's sausage, friend, and mash.

Sausage and mash,
Sausage and mash,
Hope of the hungry and joy of the just!
Sausage and mash
(Not haddock or hash),
Done till they bubble and done till they bust!
Your truffles are toys,
Your oysters are trash
Contrasted, my boys,
With the homelier joys,
The beauty, the poise,
Of sausage and mash.

A.P. Herbert

The Tryst

Potato was deep in the dark under ground,
  Tomato, above in the light.
The little tomato was ruddy and round,
  The little potato was white.

And redder and redder she rounded above.
  And paler and paler he grew,
And neither suspected a mutual love
  Till they met in a Brunswick stew.

John B. Tabb

O I C

I'm in a 10der mood today
    & feel poetic, 2;
4 fun I'll just – off a line
    & send it off 2 U.

I'm sorry you've been 6 0 long;
    Don't B disconsol8;
But bear your ills with 42de,
    And they won't Cm so gr8.

                Anon.

Skin

What should we do without our skin?
How could we keep our insides in?
If we'd no skin you cannot doubt
Our insides would keep falling out
And, ankle-deep upon the floor,
We'd paddle round in guts and gore.
O, Praise the Lord! who did invent
Our waterproof integument.

                John Sweetman

The Concrete Poem

What is a Concrete poem?
It doesn't sound quite right,
For concrete's rather heavy
And words are rather light.

Let's say you write a poem –
'Ode to a concrete slab' –
A subject none too pretty,
Which many would call drab.

Perhaps you could describe it
As full of strength and grace
And muse on what high tower
Might rest upon that base.

You may contrast its texture
With wood and weathered stone
And wonder if it will some day
Be mellowed, creeper-grown.

But if you set the words out
And shape your poem, too,
To be the slab's three faces
With each face seen askew,

So that the poem's reader
Can look as well as hear,
Why then, your final poem
Is Concrete – is that clear?

Noel Petty

Wake

Tell all my mourners
To mourn in red –
'Cause there ain't no sense
In my bein' dead.

Langston Hughes

Time for some stories

'I'll tell you a story
Of Jack-anory.
Shall I begin it?
That's all that's in it.'

Anon.

The River's Tale

(Prehistoric)

Twenty bridges from Tower to Kew
Wanted to know what the River knew,
For they were young and the Thames was old,
And this is the tale that the River told:

'I walk my beat before London Town,
Five hours up and seven down.
Up I go till I end my run
At Tide-end-town, which is Teddington.
Down I come with the mud in my hands
And plaster it over the Maplin Sands.
But I'd have you know that these waters of mine
Were once a branch of the River Rhine,
When hundreds of miles to the East I went
And England was joined to the Continent.

I remember the bat-winged lizard-birds,
The Age of Ice and the mammoth herds,
And the giant tigers that stalked them down
Through Regent's Park into Camden Town.
And I remember like yesterday
The earliest Cockney who came my way,
When he pushed through the forest that lined the
  Strand,
With paint on his face and a club in his hand.
He was death to feather and fin and fur.
He trapped my beavers at Westminster.
He netted my salmon, he hunted my deer,
He killed my heron off Lambeth Pier.
He fought his neighbour with axes and swords,
Flint or bronze, at my upper fords,
While down at Greenwich, for slaves and tin,
The tall Phoenician ships stole in,

And North Sea war-boats, painted and gay,
Flashed like dragon-flies, Erith way;
And Norseman and Negro and Gaul and Greek
Drank with the Britons in Barking Creek,
And life was gay, and the world was new,
And I was a mile across at Kew!
But the Roman came with a heavy hand,
And bridged and roaded and ruled the land,
And the Roman left and the Danes blew in –
And that's where your history-books begin!'

Rudyard Kipling

The Hippopotamus's Birthday

He has opened all his parcels
    but the largest and the last;
His hopes are at their highest
    and his heart is beating fast.
O happy Hippopotamus,
    what lovely gift is here?
He cuts the string. The world stands still.
    A pair of boots appear!

O little Hippopotamus,
    the sorrows of the small!
He dropped two tears to mingle
    with the flowing Senegal;
And the 'Thank you' that he uttered
    was the saddest ever heard
In the Senegambian jungle
    from the mouth of beast or bird.

E.V. Rieu

Dame Duck's First Lecture on Education

Old Mother Duck has hatched a brood
  Of ducklings, small and callow:
Their little wings are short, their down
  Is mottled grey and yellow.

There is a quiet little stream,
  That runs into the moat,
Where tall green sedges spread their leaves,
  And water-lilies float.

Close by the margin of the brook
  The old duck made her nest,
Of straw, and leaves, and withered grass,
  And down from her own breast.

And there she sat for four long weeks,
  In rainy days and fine,
Until the ducklings all came out –
  Four, five, six, seven, eight, nine!

One peeped out from beneath her wing,
  One scrambled on her back;
'That's very rude,' said old Dame Duck,
  'Get off! quack, quack, quack, quack!'

''Tis close,' said Dame Duck, shoving out
  The egg-shells with her bill;
'Besides, it never suits young ducks
  To keep them sitting still.'

So, rising from her nest, she said,
  'Now, children, look at me:
A well-bred duck should waddle so,
  From side to side – d'ye see?'

'Yes,' said the little ones, and then
    She went on to explain:
'A well-bred duck turns in its toes
    As I do – try again.'

'Yes,' said the ducklings, waddling on:
    'That's better,' said their mother;
'But well-bred ducks walk in a row,
    Straight – one behind another.'

'Yes,' said the little ducks again,
  All waddling in a row:
'Now to the pond,' said old Dame Duck –
  Splash, splash! and in they go.

'Let me swim first,' said old Dame Duck,
  'To this side, now to that;
There, snap at those great brown-winged flies,
  They make young ducklings fat.

'Now when you reach the poultry yard
　The hen-wife, Molly Head,
Will feed you, with the other fowls,
　On bran and mashed-up bread;

'The hens will peck and fight, but mind,
　I hope that all of you
Will gobble up the food as fast
　As well-bred ducks should do.

'You'd better get into the dish,
　Unless it is too small;
In that case I should use my foot,
　And overturn it all.'

The ducklings did as they were bid,
　And found the plan so good,
That, from that day, the other fowls
　Got hardly any food.

Aunt Effie

Zippety-Doo

There was once a man who could execute
Zippety-Doo on the yellow flute,
And several other tunes, to boot,
But he couldn't make a penny with his tootle-ti-toot!
Tootle-ootle-ootle,
      Tootle-ti-toot!

One day he met with a sing-u-lar,
Quaint old man with a big tu-ba,
Who said he'd wandered near and far,
But he couldn't make a penny with his oompa-pah!
Oompa-oompa-oompapah,
Tootle-ootle-ootle,
      Oompa-pah!

They met two men who were travelling
With a big bass drum and a cymbal thing,
Who said they'd banged since early spring,
But they couldn't make a penny with their boom-
zing-zing!

Boom-zing, boom-zing, boom-zing-zing,
Tootle-ootle-oompah,
Boom-zing-zing!

SO! the man with the flute went 'Tootle-ti-toot',
And the other man, he went 'Oompah',
And the men with the drum and the cymbal thing,
Went 'Boom-boompety-boom-boom – Zing-zing!'

And, oh, the pennies that the people fling
When they hear the tootle-oompah-boom-zing-zing!
Boom-zing, boom-zing, boom-zing-zing!
Tootle-ootle-oompah,
Boom-zing-zing!

Anon.

The Day After

I went to school
the day after Dad died.
Teacher knew all about it.
She put a hand on my shoulder
      and sighed.

In class things seemed much the same
although I felt strangely subdued,
playtime was the same too
and at lunchtime the usual crew
played-up the dinner supervisors.
Fraggle was downright rude.
I joined in the football game

but volunteered to go in goal.
That way I was left almost alone,
could think things over on my own.
For once I let the others shout
      and race and roll.

*

First thing that afternoon,
everyone in his and her place
for silent reading,
I suddenly felt hot tears streaming
      down my face.

Salty tears splashed down
and soaked into my book's page.
Sobs heaved in my chest.
Teacher peered over her half specs
and said quietly, '*Ben, come here.*'
I stood at her desk, *crying*. At my age!
I felt like an idiot, a clown.

'Don't feel ashamed,' teacher said,
'it's only right to weep.
Here, have these tissues to keep.'
I dabbed my eyes, then looked around.
        Bowed into books, every head.

          *

'Have a cold drink.
Go with James. He'll understand.'
In the boys' cloaks I drank deeply
then slowly wiped my mouth
        on the back of my hand.

Sheepishly I said, *'My dad died.'*
'I know,' said James.
'We'd best get back to class. Come on.'
Walking down the corridor I thought of Dad . . .
                      gone.

In class no one sniggered,
they were busy getting changed for games.
No one noticed I'd cried.

All day I felt sad, sad.
After school I reached my street,
clutching the tissues, dragging my feet.
Mum was there in our house,
        but no Dad, no Dad.

Wes Magee

The Pied Piper of Hamelin

I

Hamelin Town's in Brunswick,
   By famous Hanover city;
The river Weser, deep and wide,
Washes its wall on the southern side;
A pleasanter spot you never spied;
   But, when begins my ditty,
Almost five hundred years ago,
To see the townsfolk suffer so
   From vermin, was a pity.

II

   Rats!
They fought the dogs and killed the cats,
   And bit the babies in the cradles,
And ate the cheese out of the vats,
   And licked the soup from the cooks' own ladles,
Split open the kegs of salted sprats,
Made nests inside men's Sunday hats,
And even spoiled the women's chats
      By drowning their speaking
      With shrieking and squeaking
In fifty different sharps and flats.

At last the people in a body
  To the Town Hall came flocking:
''Tis clear,' cried they, 'our Mayor's a noddy;
  And as for our Corporation – shocking
To think we buy gowns lined with ermine
For dolts that can't or won't determine
What's best to rid us of our vermin!
You hope, because you're old and obese,
To find in the furry civic robe ease?
Rouse up, sirs! Give your brains a racking
To find the remedy we're lacking,
Or, sure as fate, we'll send you packing!'
At this the Mayor and Corporation
Quaked with a mighty consternation.

IV

An hour they sat in council,
   At length the Mayor broke silence:
'For a guilder I'd my ermine gown sell,
   I wish I were a mile hence!
It's easy to bid one rack one's brain –
I'm sure my poor head aches again,
I've scratched it so, and all in vain.
Oh for a trap, a trap, a trap!'
Just as he said this, what should hap
At the chamber door but a gentle tap? . . .

Robert Browning

. . . If you want to read how the story ended
   And who was knocking at the door,
   And how he looked, and what he wore,
   And what became of the city's rats
And what the mayor and the other men did,
   Told with great vigour and 'thisses and thats',
And curious rhythm and verbal clowning,
Then find a copy of Robert Browning . . .

Editor

Chicken dinner

Mama, don' do it, please
Don' cook that chicken fe dinner,
We know that chicken from she hatch
She is the only one in the batch
That the mangoose didn't catch,
Please don' cook her fe dinner.

Mama, don' do it, please,
Don' cook that chicken fe dinner,
Yuh mean to tell me yuh feget
Yuh promise her to we as a pet?
She not even have a chance fe lay yet
And yuh want fe cook her fe dinner.

Mama, don' do it, please,
Don' cook that chicken fe dinner,
Don' give Henrietta the chop,
I tell yuh what, we could swop
We will get yuh one from the shop
If yuh promise not to cook her fe dinner.

Mama, me really glad yuh know
That yuh never cook Henny fe dinner,
And she really glad too, I bet,
Oh, Lawd, me suddenly feel upset.
Yuh don' suppose is somebody else pet
We eating now fe dinner?

Valerie Bloom

Unwillingly to School

Distracted, the mother said to her boy,
'Do you try to upset and perplex and annoy?
Now, give me four reasons – and don't play the
fool –
Why you shouldn't get up and get ready for school.'

Her son replied slowly, 'Well, Mother, you see,
I can't stand the teachers and they detest me;
And there isn't a boy or a girl in the place
That I like or, in turn, that delights in my face.'

'And I'll give you two reasons,' she said, 'why you
ought
Get yourself off to school before you get caught;
Because, first, you are forty and, next, you young
fool,
It's your job to be there.
You're the head of the school.'

Gregory Harrison

A Tale of Two Citizens

I have a Russian friend who lives in Minsk
And wears a lofty hat of beaver skinsk
(Which does not suit a man so tall and thinsk).
He has a frizzly beard upon his chinsk.
He keeps his britches up with safety pinsk.
   'They're so much better than those thingsk
   Called belts and brackies, don't you thinksk?'
   You'll hear him say, the man from Minsk.

He has a Polish pal who's from Gdansk,
Who lives by selling drinksk to football fansk,
And cheese rolls, from a little caravansk.
(He finds it pleasanter than robbing banksk).
He also uses pinsk to hold his pantsk.
   'Keep up one's pantsk with rubber bandsk?!
   It can't be donesk! It simply can'tsk!
   Not in Gdansk!' he'll say. 'No thanksk!'

They're so alikesk that strangers often thinksk
That they are brothers, yesk, or even twinsk.
'I live in Minsk but I was born in Omsk,'
Says one. His friend replies, 'That's where *I'm*
                          fromsk!
Perhapsk we're brothers after all, not friendsk.'
   So they wrote homesk and asked their mumsk
   But found they weren'tsk; so they shook handsk
   And left for Minsk, and for Gdansk.

Gerard Benson

Waste

I had written to Aunt Maud,
Who was on a trip abroad,
When I heard she'd died of cramp,
Just too late to save the stamp.

Harry Graham

Wolf

'The wolf is coming!
The wolf is coming!'
the young girl said.

'Run,' said her mother.
'Run, run, or else
we'll both be dead!'

'The wolf is coming!
The wolf is coming!'
the young girl said.

'It's all right,' said her mother.
'It's got Grandma instead!'

George Murphy

Birds and beasts great and small

Great fleas have smaller fleas
    And smaller fleas to bite 'em,
And smaller fleas and smaller fleas
    And so *ad infinitum*.

                    Anon.

Two Old Crows

Two old crows sat on a fence rail.
Two old crows sat on a fence rail,
Thinking of effect and cause,
Of weeds and flowers,
And nature's laws.
One of them muttered, one of them stuttered,
One of them stuttered, one of them muttered.
Each of them thought far more than he uttered.
One crow asked the other crow a riddle.
One crow asked the other crow a riddle:
The muttering crow
Asked the stuttering crow,
'Why does a bee have a sword to his fiddle?
Why does a bee have a sword to his fiddle?'
'Bee-cause,' said the other crow,
'Bee-cause,
B B B B B B B B B B B B B B B-cause.'
Just then a bee flew close to their rail:
'Buzzzzzzzzzzzzzzzzzz zzzzzzzzz zzzzzzzzzzzzz
    ZZZZZZZ.'
And those two black crows
Turned pale,
And away those crows did sail.
Why?
B B B B B B B B B B B B B B B-cause.
B B B B B B B B B B B B B B B-cause.
'Buzzzzzzzzzzzzzzzzzz zzzzzzzzz zzzzzzzzzzzzz
    ZZZZZZZ.'

Vachel Lindsay

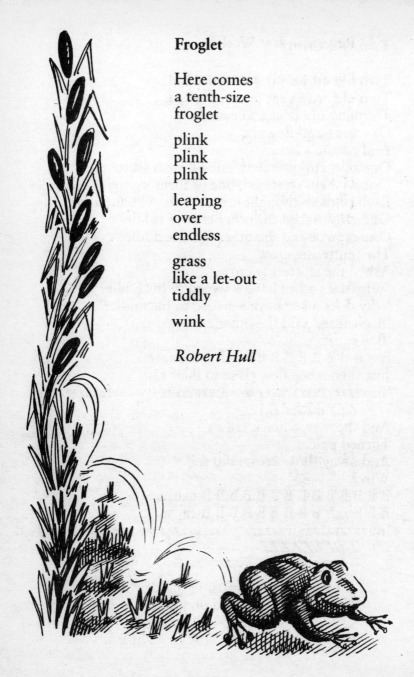

Froglet

Here comes
a tenth-size
froglet

plink
plink
plink

leaping
over
endless

grass
like a let-out
tiddly

wink

Robert Hull

Reverie in Rat Week

I want to talk about the Rat.

You've heard me talk of this and that.
Just for a change I'd like to speak
Some words about the Rat this week.

The Rat is different from the Cat,
He dare not sit upon the mat;
He sees with anxious eyes the feline,
And for his hole he makes a bee-line.

And yet he differs from the Bee,
He does not give us honey, see?

And then again, he's fond of cheese,
A food that is not liked by bees.

The Rat's a rodent beast – his habits
In this respect are like the Rabbit's.

However, in a stew, I feel,
The Rabbit makes a nicer meal.

The Rat is different from the Rhino.
You ask me why? I'm damned if I know.

He differs from the Hippo, too,
I find that very odd, don't you?

The Rat is different from the Cat . . .
I think I may have mentioned that.

I do not like this quadruped,
I feel that he is better dead.

It would not be a serious loss for us
If all his family dined on phosphorus.

A.R.D. Fairburn

The Moo-Cow-Moo

My pa held me up to the moo-cow-moo
So close I could almost touch:
An' I fed him a couple of times or two
An' I wasn't a 'fraid-cat much.

But, ef my pa goes into the house
An' ef my mamma goes too,
I jest keep still like a little mouse
'Cause the moo-cow-moo might moo!

The moo-cow-moo has a tail like a rope,
An' it's ravelled down where it grows,
An' it's jest like feelin' a piece of soap
All over the moo-cow's nose.

The moo-cow-moo has lots of fun
Jest swingin' its tail about,
But ef he opens his mouth, I run
'Cause that's where the moo comes out.

The moo-cow-moo has deers on its head
An' his eyes bog out of their place:
An' the nose of the moo-cow-moo is spread
All over the end of his face.

An' his feet is nothing but finger-nails
An' his momma don't keep them cut
An' he gives folks milk in water-pails
Ef he don't keep his handles shut.

'Cause ef you or me pulls them handles, why
The moo-cow-moo says it hurts
But our hired man he sets close by
An' squirts an' squirts an' squirts.

Edmund Vance Cook

Riddle

Four stiff standers,
Four lily-landers,
  Two lookers,
  Two crookers,
And a wig-wag!

Traditional

Lay Not Up

The bees
Sneeze and wheeze
     Scraping pollen and honey
From the lime trees:

The ants
Hurries and pants
     Storing up everything
They wants:

But the flies
Is wise
     When the cold weather comes
They dies.

L.W. Grensted

The Snake

I hate the snake
I hate the snake
I hate the way it trails and writhes
And slithers on its belly in the dirty dirt and creeps
I hate the snake
I hate its beady eye that never sleeps.

I love the snake
I love the snake
I love the way it pours and glides
And esses through the desert and loops necklaces
    on trees
I love the snake
Its zigs and zags, its ins and outs, its ease.

I hate the snake
I hate the snake
I hate its flickering liquorice tongue
Its hide and sneak, its hissiness, its picnic-wrecking
  spite
I hate its yawn
Its needle fangs, their glitter and their bite.

  I love the snake
  I love the snake
  I love its coiled elastic names
  Just listen to them: hamadryad, bandy-bandy,
     ladder,
  Sidewinder, asp
  And moccasin and fer de lance and adder

And cascabel
And copperhead
Green mamba, coachwhip, indigo –
So keep your fluffy kittens and your puppy-dogs,
   I'll take
The boomslang and
The anaconda. Oh, I love the snake!

                              Richard Edwards

Mississippi Alligator

Like a lumpy log on the limpid river,
floating near green forest bank,
pushing string-weed with a shiver,
where ferns drip heavy with the damp;
Mississippi alligator,
on the move again.

Summer rain makes water patterns,
turning, swinging water-wheels.
Round the houseboat's swaying lanterns
moths are dancing Irish reels;
Mississippi alligator,
on the move again.

Underneath the harvest moon,
rabbits' whiskers twitch and quiver.
Silent motion in the gloom,
breaks reflections on the river;
Mississippi alligator,
on the move again.

Robin Mellor

Curious Creatures

The Booglum walks at such a pace
   You haven't time to see his face,
But I have heard his face is such
   It doesn't matter very much.

The Wugg has never once been caught
   Or hunted down, like bears, for sport.
His stratagem is plain but sound –
   He hibernates the whole year round.

The Squish is such a risky pet
   Because she tends to make things wet.
One gentle squeeze or careless cuddle
   And you'll be sitting in a puddle.

The knowledgeable Aligaypus
   Makes her bed from old newspapers.
Between new sheets she likes to creep
   And read before she goes to sleep.

Tony Turner

Owl

Two radar tufts instead of ears,
Two golden globes for eyes,
Two silent sails that tell no tales,
The owl is Death's disguise.

Frank McDonald

Woodpecker

Great spotted Woodpecker –
Animated Black & Decker
In decorative blacks and whites,
Drilling holes to dig out mites.

Peter Norman

Bat

Seeker of moths with sonic wave
Slicing the dusk between church and grave;
Bat, witch-bird, seldom heard,
A shadow in flight, the swallow of night.

Catherine Benson

Mouse's Nest

I found a ball of grass among the hay
And progged it as I passed and went away;
And when I looked I fancied something stirred,
And turned agen, and hoped to catch the bird –
When out an old mouse bolted in the wheats
With all her young ones hanging at her teats;
She looked so odd and so grotesque to me,
I ran and wondered what the thing could be,
And pushed the knapweed bunches where I stood.
Then the mouse hurried from the craking brood,
The young ones squeaked, and as I went away,
She found her nest again among the hay.
The water o'er the pebbles scarce could run,
And broad old cesspools glittered in the sun.

John Clare

A Three-Toed Tree Toad's Ode

A tree toad loved a she toad
   That lived high in a tree.
She was a two-toed tree toad
But a three-toed toad was he.

The three-toed tree toad tried to win
   The she toad's nuptial nod;
For the three-toed tree toad loved the road
The two-toed tree toad trod.

Hard as the three-toed tree toad tried,
   He could not reach her limb.
From her tree toad bower, with her V-toe power
The she toad vetoed him.

Anon.

PS
Small fleas have bigger fleas
   And bigger fleas to go on,
And bigger fleas and bigger fleas
   And bigger fleas, and so on.

Anon.

Moonshine and dream-dust

If there were dreams to sell,
Merry and sad to tell,
And the crier rang the bell,
  What would you buy?

T. L. Beddoes

Dream-Dust

Gather out of star-dust
 Earth-dust,
 Cloud-dust,
 Storm-dust,
And splinters of hail,
One handful of dream-dust
 Not for sale.

    Langston Hughes

You've Wounded the Sky

'You've wounded the sky'
The child cried
As he woke from his sleep.
'You told us lies,
And you wounded the sky'
He said again, and began to weep.
When his mother asked him 'Why
Did you say what you said?'
He could only reply
'You've wounded the sky,
And soon it will be dead.
And soon we'll all be dead'.

Leo Aylen

The Land of Counterpane

When I was sick and lay a-bed,
I had two pillows at my head,
And all my toys beside me lay
To keep me happy all the day.

And sometimes for an hour or so
I watched my leaden soldiers go,
With different uniforms and drills,
Among the bed-clothes, through the hills;

And sometimes sent my ships in fleets
All up and down among the sheets;
Or brought my trees and houses out,
And planted cities all about.

I was the giant great and still
That sits upon the pillow-hill,
And sees before him, dale and plain,
The pleasant land of counterpane.

Robert Louis Stevenson

A Visit from Abroad

A speck went blowing up against the sky
   As little as a leaf: then it drew near
And broadened. – 'It's a bird,' said I,
   And fetched my bow and arrows. It was queer!
It grew from up a speck into a blot,
   And squattered past a cloud; then it flew down
All crumply, and waggled such a lot
   I thought the thing would fall. – It was a brown
Old carpet where a man was sitting snug
   Who, when he reached the ground, began to sew
A big hole in the middle of the rug,
   And kept on peeping everywhere to know
Who might be coming – then he gave a twist
   And flew away . . . I fired at him but missed.

James Stephens

London City

I have London, London, London –
all the city, small and pretty,
in a dome that's on my desk, a little dome.
I have Nelson on his column
and Saint Martin-in-the-Fields
and I have the National Gallery
and two trees,
and that's what London is – the five of these.

I can make it snow in London
when I shake the sky of London;
I can hold the little city small and pretty in my hand;
then the weather's fair in London,
in Trafalgar Square in London,
when I put my city down and let it stand.

Russell Hoban

from **The Princess**

The splendour falls on castle walls
   And snowy summits old in story:
The long light shakes across the lakes,
   And the wild cataract leaps in glory.
Blow, bugle, blow, set the wild echoes flying,
Blow, bugle; answer, echoes, dying, dying, dying.

O hark, O hear! how thin and clear,
   And thinner, clearer, farther, going!
O sweet and far from cliff and scar
   The horns of Elfland faintly blowing!
Blow, let us hear the purple glens replying:
Blow, bugle; answer, echoes, dying, dying, dying.

O love, they die in yon rich sky,
   They faint on hill or field or river:
Our echoes roll from soul to soul,
   And grow for ever and for ever.
Blow, bugle, blow, set the wild echoes flying,
And answer, echoes, answer, dying, dying, dying.

                         Alfred, Lord Tennyson

Leave Her Alone

Before today
she would like the sky to be green please
the moon to turn into bean cheese
the world to be swept by a clean breeze
    and Them to leave her alone.

Before today
she would like to pray to an old tree
the sun to bathe in the cold sea
the world to embark on a bold spree
    and Them to leave her alone.

Before today
she would like to beg with a new bowl
the swans to sing for her blue soul
the world to reach out for the true goal
    and Them to leave her alone.

Before today
she would like to rage on the sad height
laugh at the sound of the mad light
sink in the cool of a glad night
    and be forgotten, forgotten.

Martin Doyle

Foxgloves

Foxgloves on the moon keep to dark caves.
They come out at the dark of the moon only and in
waves
Swarm through the moon-towns and wherever
there's a chink
Slip into the houses and spill all the money, clink-
clink,
And crumple the notes and rearrange the silver
dishes,
And dip hands into the goldfish bowls and stir the
goldfishes,
And thumb the edges of the mirrors, and touch the
sleepers
Then at once vanish into the far distance with a wild
laugh leaving the house smelling faintly of
Virginia Creepers.

Ted Hughes

Up in the Attic . . .

(and . . . something's . . . stirring . . .)

in the dark
in the dust
boxed Christmas lights
big tooth from a shark
sad rocking horse
a model Noah's Ark
cobwebby comics
doll's house painted green
dusty wine bottles
a bust of the Queen
leather-bound books
old sewing machine
Up in the attic

and . . . Down in the Cellar . . .

Down in the cellar
brown boot in a box
remains of a cot
two brass mantel clocks
buckets and brushes
and musty old socks
damp pile of coal
and a splintered pine door
rusty rat trap
and a snaggle-toothed saw
six mildewy blankets
piled on the
stone floor

(and . . . something's . . . breathing . . .)

Wes Magee

Somewhere in the Sky

Somewhere
In the sky,
There's a door painted blue,
With a big brass knocker seven feet high.
If you can find it,
Knock, and go through –
That is, if you dare.
You'll see behind it
The secrets of the universe piled on a chair
Like a tangle of wool.
A voice will say,
'You have seven centuries in which to unwind it.
But whatever
You do,
You must never,
Ever,
Lose your temper and pull.'

Leo Aylen

Titania's Lullaby

You spotted snakes with double tongue,
   Thorny hedgehogs be not seen;
Newts and blindworms, do no wrong;
   Come not near our Fairy Queen.

     Philomel with melody,
     Sing in our sweet lullaby;
Lulla, lulla, lullaby; lulla, lulla, lullaby.
     Never harm
     Nor spell nor charm
    Come our lovely lady nigh.
    So good night, with lullaby.

Weaving spiders, come not here;
   Hence, you long-legged spinners, hence;
Beetles black, approach not near;
   Worm nor snail do no offence.

     Philomel with melody,
     Sing in our sweet lullaby;
Lulla, lulla, lullaby; lulla, lulla, lullaby.
     Never harm
     Nor spell nor charm
    Come our lovely lady nigh.
    So good night, with lullaby.

                William Shakespeare

Heaven

Heaven is
The place where
Happiness is
Everywhere.

Animals
And birds sing –
As does
Everything.

To each stone
'How-do-you-do?'
Stone answers back,
'Well! And you?'

Langston Hughes

Poets obeying the rules

True ease in writing comes by art not chance,
As those move easiest who have learned to dance.

Alexander Pope

Four distychs: complete poems of two lines

Epigram Engraved on the Collar of a Dog which I Gave to His Royal Highness

I am his Highness' dog at Kew;
Pray tell me, sir, whose dog are you?

Alexander Pope

Medieval Proverb

When the cat winketh
Little knows the mouse what the cat thinketh.

Anon.

On the Tomb of a Dentist

Stranger, approach this spot with gravity,
John Brown is filling his last cavity.

Anon.

Fishing Boats in Martigues

Around the quays, kicked off in twos
The Four Winds dry their wooden shoes.

Roy Campbell

from A Moral Alphabet

D

The Dreadful Dinotherium he
Will have to do his best for D.
The early world observed with awe
His back, indented like a saw.
His look was gay, his voice was strong;
His tail was neither short nor long;
His trunk, or elongated nose,
Was not so large as some suppose;
His teeth, as all the world allows,
Were graminivorous, like a cow's.
He therefore should have wished to pass
Long peaceful nights upon the Grass,
But being mad the brute preferred
To roost in branches, like a bird.*
A creature heavier than a whale,
You see at once, could hardly fail
To suffer badly when he slid
And tumbled (as he always did).
His fossil, therefore comes to light
All broken up: and serve him right.

   MORAL:
If you were born to walk the ground,
Remain there; do not fool around.

Hilaire Belloc

* *We have good reason to suppose*
He did so, from his claw-like toes.

Heroic couplets

from The Rape of the Lock

A Game of Cards

Behold, four Kings in majesty revered,
With hoary whiskers and a forky beard;
And four fair Queens, whose hands sustain a flower,
Th'expressive emblem of their softer power;
Four Knaves in garbs succinct, a trusty band;
Caps on their heads, and halberts in their hand;
And particolour'd troops, a shining train,
Draw forth to combat on the velvet plain.
   The skilful nymph reviews her force with care:
'Let Spades be Trumps!' she said, and Trumps they
were.

Alexander Pope

Remember

Remember me when I am gone away,
   Gone far away into the silent land;
   When you can no more hold me by the hand,
Nor I half turn to go yet turning stay.
Remember me when no more day by day
   You tell me of our future that you plann'd:
   Only remember me; you understand
It will be late to counsel then or pray.
Yet if you should forget me for a while
   And afterwards remember, do not grieve:
   For if the darkness and corruption leave
   A vestige of the thoughts that once I had,
Better by far you should forget and smile
   Than that you should remember and be sad.

Christina Rossetti

Wild Flower

Our uncut lawn to me alone brings joy,
With shaggy dandelion suns, grass bound;
To me they are not weeds, do not annoy,
Each ragged clump of leaves with light seems
                                    crowned.
I cannot understand my father's haste
To weekend mow and sever every head;
Though pleasing him, it leaves a barren waste,
A bare expanse of green, where once was spread
An emerald carpet buttoned down with gold.
So it looks now, with here and there a cloud
Of softest grey as tawny heads grow old.
Unseen I pluck each clock and laugh aloud.
I know, of course, they do not tell the hour,
But breath-blown seeds will fall, take root . . .
                            and flower!

Catherine Benson

A villanelle

Advice to Poets

If you lack an inventive brain
Writing a poem is hell.
Choose a form that has a refrain,

Then the subsequent stanzas' strain
You'll be able to bear fairly well.
If you lack an inventive brain

Before (as I'm trying to explain)
Even starting your doggerel
Choose a form that has a refrain.

Forms help to keep poets sane
(A good one's the villanelle
If you lack an inventive brain),

For most poets compose with pain
And this tip will some pain dispel –
Choose a form that has a refrain.

Get one line or, preferably, twain;
Go on ringing them like a bell:
If you lack an inventive brain
Choose a form. That has a refrain.

Roy Fuller

I Love You, My Lord

'I love you, my lord!'
    Was all that she said –
What a dissonant chord,
'I love you, my lord!'
Ah! how I abhorred
    That sarcastic maid! –
'*I* love *you*? My *Lord*!'
    Was all that she said.

                    Paul T. Gilbert

Note on Ecclesiastes

Under the sun
   There's nothing new;
Poem or pun,
Under the sun,
Said Solomon,
   And he said true.
Under the sun
   There's nothing new.

Anon.

A pantoum: two lines from each verse move down into the next

The bluebottle pantoum

The bluebottle is buzzing round the bathroom
as angry and irritated as I am
listening to its crazy one-note tune.
The window's open. Go on, scram!

As angry and as irritated as I am,
I'm trying to be helpful – look here, fly,
the window's open. Go on, scram!
Stop droning on and use your eyes.

I'm trying to be helpful – look here, fly
a little to the left, then up. And please
stop droning on and use your eyes.
Do I have to beg you on my knees?

A little left, then up and out. Please.
I'm getting close to a murder most foul.
Do I have to beg you? On my knees
my hands are clenched upon a heavy towel.

I'm getting close to a murder most foul
listening to its crazy one-note tune.
My hands are clenched upon a heavy towel.
The bluebottle is buzzing round the bathroom.

Dave Calder

The Burns Stanza

For ilka Scot wha pens a ditty
And seeks tae moralize a bittie
There is a stanza (more's the pity!)
          Wha gaes like this.
Sin' only Burns could make it witty,
          They ca'ed it his.

The Burns or Scottish stanza's sure
Tae find a place in literature;
Like haggis tae the epicure
          It's truly Scots:
It reeks o' mountain, loch, and moor
          Tae patriots.

Och, Sassenachs wil ca' it cliquey
An' say its best-laid schemes are creaky;
Let them be generous, no' cheeky:
          It will suffice
For praisin' kilts an' cockaleekie
          An' hailin' mice.

Paul Griffin

**from To a Mouse, on Turning Her Up in Her Nest
with the Plough, November 1785**

Wee, sleekit, cow'rin', tim'rous beastie,
O what a panic's in thy breastie!
Thou need not start away sae hasty,
                 Wi' bickering brattle!
I wad be laith to rin an' chase thee
                    Wi' murd'ring pattle . . .

Robert Burns

Limericks

There was an Old Man at a casement,
Who held up his hands in amazement;
   When they said, 'Sir, you'll fall!'
   He replied, 'Not at all!'
That incipient Old Man at a casement.

There was an Old Man of Thermopylae,
Who never did anything properly;
   But they said, 'If you choose
   To boil Eggs in your Shoes,
You shall never remain in Thermopylae.'

There was a Young Lady of Russia,
Who screamed so that no one could hush her;
   Her screams were extreme –
   No one heard such a scream
As was screamed by that Lady of Russia.

Edward Lear

The Old Lady of Ryde

There was an old lady of Ryde
Who ate some green apples and died.
   The apples fermented
   Within the lamented,
Making cider inside 'er inside.

Anon.

Fashion Note

There was a young man from The Cape
Who always wore trousers of crêpe;
   When asked, 'Don't they tear?'
   He replied, 'Here and there,
But they keep such a beautiful shape.'

Anon.

The Young Lady from Sheen

There was a young lady from Sheen
Whose musical ear was not keen:
   She said, 'It is odd,
   But I cannot tell *God*
Save the Weasel from *Pop Goes the Queen*!'

Anon.

Lim

There once was a bard of Hong Kong,
Who thought limericks were too long.

Gerard Benson

INDEX OF FIRST LINES

153

ACKNOWLEDGEMENTS

The editor and publishers gratefully acknowledge permission to reproduce copyright poems in this book:

'Racing the wind' from *Racing the Wind* by Moira Andrew, published by Nelson, 1993, reprinted by permission of the author; 'Somewhere in the Sky' from *Rhymoceros* by Leo Aylen, published by Macmillan, reprinted by permission of the author; 'You've Wounded the Sky' by Leo Aylen, copyright © by permission of the author; 'Pembroke' by William Bealby-Wright, by permission of the author and by arrangement with The Barrow Poets; 'D' from *A Moral Alphabet* by Hilaire Belloc, reprinted by permission of the Peters Fraser & Dunlop Group Ltd; 'Bat' and 'Wild Flower' by Catherine Benson, by permission of the author; 'Conversation', 'Lim', note on 'The Pied Piper of Hamelin' and 'A Tale of Two Citizens' copyright © Gerard Benson; 'Banana and Mackerel' from *When I Dance* by James Berry, copyright © James Berry, 1988, first published by Hamish Hamilton Children's Books; 'Chicken dinner' from *Duppy Jamboree* by Valerie Bloom, by permission of the publishers, Cambridge University Press; 'simple tings' taken from *Riddym Ravings and Other Poems* by Jean 'Binta' Breeze, published by Race Today publications, 165 Railton Road, London SE24 0LU (1988), ISBN 0–947716–14–9, £3.50 paperback; 'The bluebottle pantoum' by Dave Calder, by permission of the author; 'Fishing Boats in Martigues' by Roy Campbell, by kind permission of Teresa Campbell; 'The Wide-Eyed Stride Poem' by Tony Charles, by permission of the author; 'Who Unplugged the Fridge?' by John Coldwell, by permission of the author; 'Leave Her Alone' by Martin Doyle, by permission of the author; 'The Snake' from *The House That Caught a Cold* by Richard Edwards, copyright © Richard Edwards, 1991, first published by Viking; 'Reverie in Rat Week' from *Collected Poems* by A.R.D. Fairburn, by permission of the Richards Literary Agency, Auckland, NZ; 'Who?' and 'Advice to Poets' from *The World Through the Window* by Roy Fuller, copyright © Roy Fuller, 1972, 1977, 1982 & 1989, first published by Blackie & Son Ltd; 'Frying Panic' by Bill Greenwell, by permission of the author; 'The Burns Stanza' from *How to be Well-Versed in Poetry*, published by Viking, editor E.O. Parrott, copyright © Paul Griffin, by permission of